SIMPLE MACHINES

wheels & axles

VALERIE BODDEN

Published by Creative Education
P.O. Box 227, Mankato, Minnesota 56002
Creative Education is an imprint of The Creative Company
www.thecreativecompany.us

Design and production by Liddy Walseth
Art direction by Rita Marshall
Printed by Corporate Graphics in the United States of America

Photographs by Dreamstime (Arun Bhargava, John Blanton, Farek),
Getty Images (Walter Bibikow, Peter deLory, Shannon Fagan, Hulton Archive,
Douglas Miller, Tim Robberts, SuperStock, Robert Van Der Hilst, Ken Welsh),
iStockphoto (Olaf Bender, Kevin Bergen, Ben Conlan, Paul Flemming,
Javier Fontanella, Londa Freeman, William Sherman)

Library of Congress Cataloging-in-Publication Data
Bodden, Valerie.
Wheels & axles / by Valerie Bodden.
p. cm. — (Simple machines)
Summary: A foundational look at wheels and axles, explaining how these simple
machines work and describing some common examples, such as doorknobs, that
have been used throughout history.
Includes index.
ISBN 978-1-60818-013-4
1. Wheels—Juvenile literature. 2. Axles—Juvenile literature. I. Title. II. Title:
Wheels and axles.
TJ181.5.B593 2011
621.8'11—dc22 2009048844
CPSIA: 040110 PO1140

First Edition
2 4 6 8 9 7 5 3 1

CREATIVE C EDUCATION

SIMPLE MACHINES

wheels & axles

VALERIE BODDEN

contents

Have you ever ridden on roller skates or turned a doorknob? You might not have known it, but you were using wheels and axles (*AK-sulz*). Wheels and axles make it easier to move objects.

A wheel and axle is a kind of simple machine. Simple machines have only a few moving parts. Some have no moving parts at all. Simple machines help people do WORK.

Wheels and axles are used in all kinds of vehicles

A wheel is flat and round. An axle is a rod that is CONNECTED to the middle of a wheel. It is not as big around as the wheel. Some axles spin when the wheel spins. Other axles stay still.

Early
wheels
were used
on small
wagons

Wheels can also make it easier to turn axles. If you want to turn on a faucet, you turn the handle (or wheel). That makes the stem (or axle) turn, too.

If you tried to turn an axle by itself, you would have to push or twist very hard. You do not have to push as hard to move a wheel. But you do have to turn the wheel farther.

Wheels and axles help many machines move

People have been using wheels and axles for thousands of years. Some of the earliest wheels were **POTTER'S WHEELS** used in Egypt. Wheels and axles were used on wagons and **CHARIOTS**, too.

Today, people still use wheels and axles. Bikes, skateboards, and cars all have wheels and axles. Merry-go-rounds and Ferris wheels are made up of wheels and axles, too!

People like riding the London Eye Ferris wheel

A doorknob is a wheel and axle. The knob is the wheel, and the bar inside the door is the axle. Even a pizza cutter is made of a wheel and axle. Wheels and axles are everywhere. Without them, we would have a much harder time moving the objects around us!

A CLOSER LOOK at
Wheels and *Axles*

IF YOU TURN A TOY WAGON UPSIDE DOWN, YOU WILL SEE

THAT IT HAS FOUR WHEELS AND TWO AXLES. SPIN THE

WHEELS. DO THE AXLES MOVE, TOO? NOW FILL A SMALL

BOX WITH ROCKS OR BOOKS. TRY PUSHING THE BOX

ACROSS THE GROUND. HOW FAR CAN YOU MOVE IT? HAVE

A GROWN-UP PUT THE BOX IN YOUR WAGON FOR YOU.

TRY TO PULL IT. NOW HOW FAR CAN YOU GO?

Glossary

chariots—vehicles used long ago; they had two wheels and were pulled by horses

connected—joined together

potter's wheels—wheels that are laid horizontally, or flat, and are spun to turn a lump of clay in a circle so that a person can form the clay into a bowl, jar, or other object

work—using force (a push or pull) to move an object

Read More

Oxlade, Chris. *Wheels.* Chicago: Heinemann Library, 2003.

Thales, Sharon. *Wheels and Axles to the Rescue.* Mankato, Minn.: Capstone Press, 2007.

Web Sites

MIKIDS.com
http://www.mikids.com/Smachines.htm
Learn about the six kinds of simple machines and see examples of each one.

Simple Machines
http://staff.harrisonburg.k12.va.us/~mwampole/1-resources/simple-machines/index.html
Try to figure out which common objects are simple machines.

Index